Meditations.
REVERB CULTURE

Meditations.
REVERB CULTURE

Meditations on Scripture and the
Catechism of the Catholic Church

Volume One

The Profession of Faith

REVERB CULTURE PRESS

Reverb Culture Press
www.ReverbCulture.com

This book was self-published by the author and editor
Edmund Mitchell under Reverb Culture Press.

Cover and interior design by Edmund Mitchell.

Published in the United States by Reverb Culture Press

ISBN: 0-9981930-0-3
ISBN-13: 978-0-9981930-0-7

DEDICATION

For Catholics who desire to sit at the feet of the Church, to soak in the truth whole and entire, to go to the sources, and to find their own way.

"Scripture is like words from my Father, and the Catechism is like words from my Mother."

— Abraham Villela

I believe in God, the Father Almighty, creator of heaven and earth. And in Jesus Christ, His only Son, our Lord. He was conceived by the power of the Holy Spirit and born of the Virgin Mary. He suffered under Pontius Pilate, was crucified, died, and was buried. He descended into Hell. On the third day He rose again. He ascended into Heaven and is seated at the right hand of the Father. He will come again to judge the living and the dead. I believe in the Holy Spirit, the holy catholic Church, the communion of saints, the forgiveness of sins, the resurrection of the body and life everlasting.
Amen.

TABLE OF CONTENTS

HOW TO USE THIS BOOK

Daily prayer changed my life. At first it was just a few minutes each day of quiet conversation with God. I felt close to God.

Then I started reading the Bible as part of my prayer. I felt I grew even closer to God. I met Jesus in the Scriptures.

But I reached a point where I felt like I was on my own.

So I'd turn to other smart and holy people to help guide me through Scripture and my relationship with Jesus. I started consuming all the great Catholic stuff out there like sermons, podcasts, books, videos, radio, talks, conferences, and devotionals.

I tended to gravitate toward my favorite devotions and areas of the faith that I felt comfortable with. It was easy to stay away from areas that I was weak in or struggled with. After a few years, I started realizing there were lots of holes in my faith. There were still areas of the Bible, the faith, my life, and even areas of my relationship with Jesus that were missing or lacking.

I felt a strong desire to go to the sources. I wanted to be guided in prayer by the Church I loved and the Scriptures where I met Jesus. I wanted to sit at the feet of the Church and be molded by Jesus into a better disciple.

This is when my understanding of the Catechism of the Catholic Church radically changed.

On October 11, 1992, on the 30th anniversary of Vatican II, the Catholic Church gave to its people and the world the Catechism of the Catholic Church. This Catechism is a definitive statement of all the Catholic Church believes and all that has been echoed down to us since the first Apostles.

It is divided into the same pillars the first Christians in Acts 2:42 devoted themselves to:

the teaching of the apostles (Creed),
the breaking of the bread (Sacraments and Liturgy),
the communal life (Morality),
and prayer.

I read twenty plus books from authors of the Catechism and experts in the field. I spent countless hours poring through the Catechism, studying it, and eventually started praying with it.

Slowly I began incorporating the Catechism into my daily prayer life. It changed everything. Through lots of trial and error and even teaching others, I developed a rhythm of praying with Scripture and the Catechism. First, I pray with a small chunk of Scripture. Then, using the Catechism's index of citations to find related Catechism passages, I pray with a related Catechism paragraph. Finally, I enter into conversation with God, meditating on the Word of God now enlightened by the teaching and authority of the

Church expressed in the Catechism. I spend time journaling out my prayer. I end my prayer resting in God and thanking Him for his Word and His Church.

This book is meant to be an easy way to pray with Scripture and the Catechism. It contains thirty short meditations on a major theme from the first pillar of the Catechism of the Catholic Church – "The Profession of Faith".

This pillar could also be referred to as the "Creed" pillar.

Pray. Each meditation builds on the previous one. By praying through all the meditations, you will be taken through the highlights of the entire "Creed" pillar of the Catechism.

These meditations would work well as daily meditations for 30 days, but feel free to spend more time with each meditation or to return to them more than once.

The numbers in bold are Scripture passages and paragraph numbers from the Catechism of the Catholic Church.

> **John 3:16.** – Scripture citation
> **436.** – Catechism paragraph number
> **Journal.** – Space for you to journal your prayer

Journal. At the end of each meditation, there is room for you to journal. You'll find extra blank journal pages at the end of the book.

Share. Share your experiences, insights, and blessings God gives you with others!

Get a few friends together and start a small group to journey together through the meditations. Meet up to pray and discuss the meditations that stood out to you and how God is speaking through these meditations. (We offer bulk discounts on quantity orders over 10.)

And we'd love for you to post a picture of you and your book or one of your journaling pages to social media. Use the hash tag:

#reverbmeditations

Sunday Gospel Readings. As an extra bonus, in the back you'll also find an index of Sunday Gospel Readings with Catechism References for the Three Year Cycle. With this, a Catechism, and a Bible, you could keep the meditations going weekly by praying through each Sunday's Gospel reading.

I hope God blessed you and I pray that you discover the pulsating heart of Scripture and the Catechism. As Father Ranierro Cantalamessa said:

"In short, we need to discover the Catechism's pulsating heart. And what is this heart? It is not a dogma or a truth, a doctrine or an ethical principle. It is a Person: Jesus Christ!"
— Fr. Raniero Cantalamessa

+J.M.J.
Edmund Mitchell
Founder, Reverb Culture

THE GOOD NEWS

Ephesians 1:3-14. Blessed be the God and Father of our Lord Jesus Christ, who has blessed us in Christ with every spiritual blessing in the heavens, as he chose us in him, before the foundation of the world, to be holy and without blemish before him.

In love he destined us for adoption to himself through Jesus Christ, …In him we have redemption by his blood, the forgiveness of transgressions, in accord with the riches of his grace that he lavished upon us. In all wisdom and insight, he has made known to us the mystery of his will in accord with his favor that he set forth in him as a plan for the fullness of times, to sum up all things in Christ, in heaven and on earth.

In him we were also chosen, destined in accord with the purpose of the One who accomplishes all things according to the intention of his will, so that we might exist for the praise of his glory, we who first hoped in Christ. In him you also, who have heard the word of truth, the gospel of your salvation, and have believed in him, were sealed with the promised holy Spirit, which is the first installment of our inheritance toward redemption as God's possession, to the praise of his glory.

1. God, infinitely perfect and blessed in himself, in a plan of sheer goodness freely created man to make him share in his own blessed life. For this reason, at every time and in every place, God draws close to man. He calls man to seek him, to know him, to love him with all his strength. He calls together all men, scattered and divided by sin, into the unity of his family, the Church. To accomplish this, when the fullness of time had come, God sent his Son as Redeemer and Savior. In his Son and through him, he invites men to become, in the Holy Spirit, his adopted children and thus heirs of his blessed life.

Journal.

Journal.

THE CATECHISM

1 John 1:1-4. What was from the beginning, what we have heard, what we have seen with our eyes, what we looked upon and touched with our hands concerns the Word of life— for the life was made visible; we have seen it and testify to it and proclaim to you the eternal life that was with the Father and was made visible to us—what we have seen and heard we proclaim now to you, so that you too may have fellowship with us; for our fellowship is with the Father and with his Son, Jesus Christ. We are writing this so that our joy may be complete.

4. Quite early on, the name catechesis was given to the totality of the Church's efforts to make disciples, to help men believe that Jesus is the Son of God so that believing they might have life in his name, and to educate and instruct them in this life, thus building up the body of Christ.

426. "At the heart of catechesis we find, in essence, a Person, the Person of Jesus of Nazareth, the only Son from the Father...who suffered and died for us and who now, after rising, is living with us forever." To catechize is "to reveal in the Person of Christ the whole of God's eternal design reaching fulfillment in that Person. It is to seek to understand the meaning of Christ's actions and words and of the signs worked by him.'" Catechesis aims at putting "people ... in communion ... with Jesus Christ: only he can lead us to the love of the Father in the Spirit and make us share in the life of the Holy Trinity."

Journal.

SEEKING GOD

Psalm 105:3-6. Glory in his holy name; let hearts that seek the Lord rejoice! Seek out the Lord and his might; constantly seek his face. Recall the wondrous deeds he has done, his wonders and words of judgment, you descendants of Abraham his servant, offspring of Jacob the chosen one!

27. The desire for God is written in the human heart, because man is created by God and for God; and God never ceases to draw man to himself. Only in God will he find the truth and happiness he never stops searching for: The dignity of man rests above all on the fact that he is called to communion with God. This invitation to converse with God is addressed to man as soon as he comes into being. For if man exists it is because God has created him through love, and through love continues to hold him in existence. He cannot live fully according to truth unless he freely acknowledges that love and entrusts himself to his creator.

30. "Let the hearts of those who seek the LORD rejoice." Although man can forget God or reject him, He never ceases to call every man to seek him, so as to find life and happiness. But this search for God demands of man every effort of intellect, a sound will, "an upright heart", as well as the witness of others who teach him to seek God.

Journal.

GOD REVEALS HIMSELF

1 Timothy 6:13-16. I charge [you] before God, who gives life to all things, and before Christ Jesus, who gave testimony under Pontius Pilate for the noble confession, to keep the commandment without stain or reproach until the appearance of our Lord Jesus Christ that the blessed and only ruler will make manifest at the proper time, the King of kings and Lord of lords, who alone has immortality, who dwells in unapproachable light, and whom no human being has seen or can see. To him be honor and eternal power. Amen.

50. By natural reason man can know God with certainty, on the basis of his works. But there is another order of knowledge, which man cannot possibly arrive at by his own powers: the order of divine Revelation. Through an utterly free decision, God has revealed himself and given himself to man. This he does by revealing the mystery, his plan of loving goodness, formed from all eternity in Christ, for the benefit of all men. God has fully revealed this plan by sending us his beloved Son, our Lord Jesus Christ, and the Holy Spirit.

Journal.

SACRED SCRIPTURE

John 1:1-5. In the beginning was the Word, and the Word was with God, and the Word was God. He was in the beginning with God. All things came to be through him, and without him nothing came to be. What came to be through him was life, and this life was the light of the human race; the light shines in the darkness, and the darkness has not overcome it.

102. Through all the words of Sacred Scripture, God speaks only one single Word, his one Utterance in whom he expresses himself completely.

103. For this reason, the Church has always venerated the Scriptures as she venerates the Lord's Body. She never ceases to present to the faithful the bread of life, taken from the one table of God's Word and Christ's Body.

104. In Sacred Scripture, the Church constantly finds her nourishment and her strength, for she welcomes it not as a human word, "but as what it really is, the word of God". "In the sacred books, the Father who is in heaven comes lovingly to meet his children, and talks with them."

Journal.

WE RESPOND

Romans 16:25-27. Now to him who can strengthen you, according to my gospel and the proclamation of Jesus Christ, according to the revelation of the mystery kept secret for long ages but now manifested through the prophetic writings and, according to the command of the eternal God, made known to all nations to bring about the obedience of faith, to the only wise God, through Jesus Christ be glory forever and ever. Amen.

142. *By his Revelation*, "the invisible God, from the fullness of his love, addresses men as his friends, and moves among them, in order to invite and receive them into his own company." The adequate response to this invitation is faith.

143. *By faith*, man completely submits his intellect and his will to God. With his whole being man gives his assent to God the revealer. Sacred Scripture calls this human response to God, the author of revelation, "the obedience of faith".

144. To obey (from the Latin *ob-audire*, to "hear or listen to") in faith is to submit freely to the word that has been heard, because its truth is guaranteed by God, who is Truth itself.

Journal.

WE BELIEVE IN GOD

Hebrews 11:1-3, 6. Faith is the realization of what is hoped for and evidence of things not seen. Because of it the ancients were well attested. By faith we understand that the universe was ordered by the word of God, so that what is visible came into being through the invisible.

But without faith it is impossible to please him, for anyone who approaches God must believe that he exists and that he rewards those who seek him.

166. Faith is a personal act — the free response of the human person to the initiative of God who reveals himself. But faith is not an isolated act. No one can believe alone, just as no one can live alone. You have not given yourself faith as you have not given yourself life. The believer has received faith from others and should hand it on to others. Our love for Jesus and for our neighbor impels us to speak to others about our faith. Each believer is thus a link in the great chain of believers. I cannot believe without being carried by the faith of others, and by my faith I help support others in the faith.

Journal.

GOD, THE TRIUNE

John 14:8-11, 15-20 Philip said to him, "Master, show us the Father, and that will be enough for us." Jesus said to him, "Have I been with you for so long a time and you still do not know me, Philip? Whoever has seen me has seen the Father. How can you say, 'Show us the Father'? Do you not believe that I am in the Father and the Father is in me? The words that I speak to you I do not speak on my own. The Father who dwells in me is doing his works. ...

"If you love me, you will keep my commandments. And I will ask the Father, and he will give you another Advocate to be with you always, the Spirit of truth, which the world cannot accept, because it neither sees nor knows it. But you know it, because it remains with you, and will be in you. I will not leave you orphans; I will come to you. In a little while the world will no longer see me, but you will see me, because I live and you will live. On that day you will realize that I am in my Father and you are in me and I in you.

230. Even when he reveals himself, God remains a mystery beyond words: "If you understood him, it would not be God"

233. Christians are baptized in the *name* of the Father and of the Son and of the Holy Spirit: not in their *names*, for there is only one God, the almighty Father, his only Son and the Holy Spirit: the Most Holy Trinity.

234. The mystery of the Most Holy Trinity is the central mystery of Christian faith and life. It is the mystery of God in himself. It is therefore the source of all the other mysteries of faith, the light that enlightens them. It is the most fundamental and essential teaching in the "hierarchy of the truths of faith". The whole history of salvation is identical with the history of the way and the means by which the one true God, Father, Son and Holy Spirit, reveals himself to men "and reconciles and unites with himself those who turn away from sin".

Journal.

Journal.

GOD, THE FATHER ALMIGHTY

Romans 8:14-17. For those who are led by the Spirit of God are children of God. For you did not receive a spirit of slavery to fall back into fear, but you received a spirit of adoption, through which we cry, "Abba, Father!" The Spirit itself bears witness with our spirit that we are children of God, and if children, then heirs, heirs of God and joint heirs with Christ, if only we suffer with him so that we may also be glorified with him.

239. By calling God "Father", the language of faith indicates two main things: that God is the first origin of everything and transcendent authority; and that he is at the same time goodness and loving care for all his children. God's parental tenderness can also be expressed by the image of motherhood, which emphasizes God's immanence, the intimacy between Creator and creature. The language of faith thus draws on the human experience of parents, who are in a way the first representatives of God for man. But this experience also tells us that human parents are fallible and can disfigure the face of fatherhood and motherhood. We ought therefore to recall that God transcends the human distinction between the sexes. He is neither man nor woman: he is God. He also transcends human fatherhood and motherhood, although he is their origin and standard: no one is father as God is Father.

Journal.

GOD, THE CREATOR

John 6:25-34. "Therefore I tell you, do not worry about your life, what you will eat [or drink], or about your body, what you will wear. Is not life more than food and the body more than clothing? Look at the birds in the sky; they do not sow or reap, they gather nothing into barns, yet your heavenly Father feeds them. Are not you more important than they? Can any of you by worrying add a single moment to your life-span? Why are you anxious about clothes? Learn from the way the wild flowers grow. They do not work or spin. But I tell you that not even Solomon in all his splendor was clothed like one of them.

If God so clothes the grass of the field, which grows today and is thrown into the oven tomorrow, will he not much more provide for you, O you of little faith? So do not worry and say, 'What are we to eat?' or 'What are we to drink?' or 'What are we to wear?' All these things the pagans seek. Your heavenly Father knows that you need them all. But seek first the kingdom [of God] and his righteousness, and all these things will be given you besides. Do not worry about tomorrow; tomorrow will take care of itself. Sufficient for a day is its own evil."

302. Creation has its own goodness and proper perfection, but it did not spring forth complete from the hands of the Creator. The universe was created "in a state of journeying" (*in statu viae*) toward an ultimate perfection yet to be attained, to which God has destined it. We call "divine providence" the dispositions by which God guides his creation toward this perfection:

By his providence God protects and governs all things which he has made, "reaching mightily from one end of the earth to the other, and ordering all things well". For "all are open and laid bare to his eyes", even those things which are yet to come into existence through the free action of creatures.

Journal.

Journal.

HEAVEN AND EARTH

Matthew 5:14-16. "You are the light of the world. A city set on a mountain cannot be hidden. Nor do they light a lamp and then put it under a bushel basket; it is set on a lampstand, where it gives light to all in the house. Just so, your light must shine before others, that they may see your good deeds and glorify your heavenly Father."

Psalm 115:16. The heavens belong to the Lord, but he has given the earth to the children of Adam.

326. The Scriptural expression "heaven and earth" means all that exists, creation in its entirety. It also indicates the bond, deep within creation, that both unites heaven and earth and distinguishes the one from the other: "the earth" is the world of men, while "heaven" or "the heavens" can designate both the firmament and God's own "place" — "our Father in heaven" and consequently the "heaven" too which is eschatological glory. Finally, "heaven" refers to the saints and the "place" of the spiritual creatures, the angels, who surround God.

Journal.

MAN

Genesis 1:26-27. Then God said: Let us make human beings in our image, after our likeness. Let them have dominion over the fish of the sea, the birds of the air, the tame animals, all the wild animals, and all the creatures that crawl on the earth.

God created mankind in his image;
in the image of God he created them;
male and female he created them.

302. Of all visible creatures only man is "able to know and love his creator". He is "the only creature on earth that God has willed for its own sake", and he alone is called to share, by knowledge and love, in God's own life. It was for this end that he was created, and this is the fundamental reason for his dignity:

"What made you establish man in so great a dignity? Certainly the incalculable love by which you have looked on your creature in yourself! You are taken with love for her;

for by love indeed you created her, by love you have given
her a being capable of tasting your eternal Good."
–St. Catherine of Siena

Journal.

ORIGINAL SIN

Genesis 3:1-7. Now the snake was the most cunning of all the wild animals that the Lord God had made. He asked the woman, "Did God really say, 'You shall not eat from any of the trees in the garden'?" The woman answered the snake: "We may eat of the fruit of the trees in the garden; it is only about the fruit of the tree in the middle of the garden that God said, 'You shall not eat it or even touch it, or else you will die.'" But the snake said to the woman: "You certainly will not die! God knows well that when you eat of it your eyes will be opened and you will be like gods, who know good and evil." The woman saw that the tree was good for food and pleasing to the eyes, and the tree was desirable for gaining wisdom. So she took some of its fruit and ate it; and she also gave some to her husband, who was with her, and he ate it. Then the eyes of both of them were opened, and they knew that they were naked; so they sewed fig leaves together and made loincloths for themselves.

390. The account of the fall in Genesis 3 uses figurative language, but affirms a primeval event, a deed that took place *at the beginning of the history of man*. Revelation gives us the certainty of faith that the whole of human history is marked by the original fault freely committed by our first parents.

397. Man, tempted by the devil, let his trust in his Creator die in his heart and, abusing his freedom, disobeyed God's command. This is what man's first sin consisted of. All subsequent sin would be disobedience toward God and lack of trust in his goodness.

Journal.

THE DEVIL

John 8:42-44. Jesus said to them, "If God were your Father, you would love me, for I came from God and am here; I did not come on my own, but he sent me. Why do you not understand what I am saying? Because you cannot bear to hear my word. You belong to your father the devil and you willingly carry out your father's desires. He was a murderer from the beginning and does not stand in truth, because there is no truth in him. When he tells a lie, he speaks in character, because he is a liar and the father of lies."

391. Behind the disobedient choice of our first parents lurks a seductive voice, opposed to God, which makes them fall into death out of envy. Scripture and the Church's Tradition see in this being a fallen angel, called "Satan" or the "devil". The Church teaches that Satan was at first a good angel, made by God: "The devil and the other demons were indeed created naturally good by God, but they became evil by their own doing."

Journal.

JESUS CHRIST – THE SON OF GOD

Matthew 3:13-17. Then Jesus came from Galilee to John at the Jordan to be baptized by him. John tried to prevent him, saying, "I need to be baptized by you, and yet you are coming to me?" Jesus said to him in reply, "Allow it now, for thus it is fitting for us to fulfill all righteousness." Then he allowed him. After Jesus was baptized, he came up from the water and behold, the heavens were opened [for him], and he saw the Spirit of God descending like a dove [and] coming upon him. And a voice came from the heavens, saying, "This is my beloved Son, with whom I am well pleased."

422. 'But when the time had fully come, God sent forth his Son, born of a woman, born under the law, to redeem those who were under the law, so that we might receive adoption as sons.' This is 'the gospel of Jesus Christ, the Son of God:' God has visited his people. He has fulfilled the promise he made to Abraham and his descendants. He acted far beyond all expectation — he has sent his own 'beloved Son'.

444. The Gospels report that at two solemn moments, the Baptism and the Transfiguration of Christ, the voice of the Father designates Jesus his "beloved Son". Jesus calls himself the "only Son of God", and by this title affirms his eternal pre-existence. He asks for faith in "the name of the only Son of God". In the centurion's exclamation before the crucified Christ, "Truly this man was the Son of God", that Christian confession is already heard. Only in the Paschal mystery can the believer give the title "Son of God" its full meaning.

Journal.

CONCEIVED BY THE POWER
OF THE HOLY SPIRIT

Luke 1:30-38 Then the angel said to her, "Do not be afraid, Mary, for you have found favor with God. Behold, you will conceive in your womb and bear a son, and you shall name him Jesus. He will be great and will be called Son of the Most High, and the Lord God will give him the throne of David his father, and he will rule over the house of Jacob forever, and of his kingdom there will be no end." But Mary said to the angel, "How can this be, since I have no relations with a man?" And the angel said to her in reply, "The holy Spirit will come upon you, and the power of the Most High will overshadow you. Therefore the child to be born will be called holy, the Son of God. ...

Mary said, "Behold, I am the handmaid of the Lord. May it be done to me according to your word." Then the angel departed from her.

484. The Annunciation to Mary inaugurates "the fullness of time", the time of the fulfillment of God's promises and preparations. Mary was invited to conceive him in whom the "whole fullness of deity" would dwell "bodily". The divine response to her question, "How can this be, since I know not man?", was given by the power of the Spirit: "The Holy Spirit will come upon you."

485. The mission of the Holy Spirit is always conjoined and ordered to that of the Son. The Holy Spirit, "the Lord, the giver of Life", is sent to sanctify the womb of the Virgin Mary and divinely fecundate it, causing her to conceive the eternal Son of the Father in a humanity drawn from her own.

Journal.

TRUE GOD AND TRUE MAN

John 1:14-18. And the Word became flesh and made his dwelling among us, and we saw his glory, the glory as of the Father's only Son, full of grace and truth.

John testified to him and cried out, saying, "This was he of whom I said, 'The one who is coming after me ranks ahead of me because he existed before me.'" From his fullness we have all received, grace in place of grace, because while the law was given through Moses, grace and truth came through Jesus Christ. No one has ever seen God. The only Son, God, who is at the Father's side, has revealed him.

464. The unique and altogether singular event of the Incarnation of the Son of God does not mean that Jesus Christ is part God and part man, nor does it imply that he is the result of a confused mixture of the divine and the human. He became truly man while remaining truly God. Jesus Christ is true God and true man. During the first centuries, the Church had to defend and clarify this truth of faith against the heresies that falsified it.

Journal.

THE LIFE OF JESUS

John 20:30-31. Now Jesus did many other signs in the presence of [his] disciples that are not written in this book. But these are written that you may [come to] believe that Jesus is the Messiah, the Son of God, and that through this belief you may have life in his name.

516. Christ's whole earthly life — his words and deeds, his silences and sufferings, indeed his manner of being and speaking — is *Revelation* of the Father. Jesus can say: "Whoever has seen me has seen the Father", and the Father can say: "This is my Son, my Chosen; listen to him!" Because our Lord became man in order to do his Father's will, even the least characteristics of his mysteries manifest "God's love... among us".

517. Christ's whole life is a mystery of *redemption*. Redemption comes to us above all through the blood of his cross, but this mystery is at work throughout Christ's entire life:

- already in his Incarnation through which by becoming poor he enriches us with his poverty;

- in his hidden life which by his submission atones for our disobedience;
- in his word which purifies its hearers;
- in his healings and exorcisms by which "he took our infirmities and bore our diseases";
- and in his Resurrection by which he justifies us.

518. Christ's whole life is a mystery of recapitulation. All Jesus did, said and suffered had for its aim restoring fallen man to his original vocation.

Journal.

JESUS DIED AND ROSE AGAIN

John 19:24-30. After this, aware that everything was now finished, in order that the scripture might be fulfilled, Jesus said, "I thirst." There was a vessel filled with common wine. So they put a sponge soaked in wine on a sprig of hyssop and put it up to his mouth. When Jesus had taken the wine, he said, "It is finished." And bowing his head, he handed over the spirit.

John 20:19-23. On the evening of that first day of the week, when the doors were locked, where the disciples were, for fear of the Jews, Jesus came and stood in their midst and said to them, "Peace be with you." When he had said this, he showed them his hands and his side. The disciples rejoiced when they saw the Lord.

618. The cross is the unique sacrifice of Christ, the "one mediator between God and men". But because in his incarnate divine person he has in some way united himself to every man, "the possibility of being made partners, in a way known to God, in the paschal mystery" is offered to all men. He calls his disciples to "take up [their] cross and follow [him]", for "Christ also suffered for [us], leaving [us] an example so that [we] should follow in his steps." In fact Jesus desires to associate with his redeeming sacrifice those who were to be its first beneficiaries. This is achieved supremely in the case of his mother, who was associated more intimately than any other person in the mystery of his redemptive suffering.

Apart from the cross there is no other ladder by which we may get to heaven. – St. Rose of Lima

647. O truly blessed Night, sings the Exultet of the Easter Vigil, which alone deserved to know the time and the hour when Christ rose from the realm of the dead! But no one was an eyewitness to Christ's Resurrection and no evangelist describes it. No one can say how it came about physically. Still less was its innermost essence, his passing over to another life, perceptible to the senses. Although the Resurrection was an historical event that could be verified by the sign of the empty tomb and by the reality of the apostles' encounters with the risen Christ, still it remains at the very heart of the mystery of faith as something that transcends and surpasses history. This is why the risen Christ does not reveal himself to the world, but to his disciples, "to those who came up with him from Galilee to Jerusalem, who are now his witnesses to the people."

Journal.

I BELIEVE IN THE HOLY SPIRIT

Acts 2:1-4. When the time for Pentecost was fulfilled, they were all in one place together. And suddenly there came from the sky a noise like a strong driving wind, and it filled the entire house in which they were. Then there appeared to them tongues as of fire, which parted and came to rest on each one of them. And they were all filled with the holy Spirit and began to speak in different tongues, as the Spirit enabled them to proclaim.

683. "No one can say 'Jesus is Lord' except by the Holy Spirit." "God has sent the Spirit of his Son into our hearts, crying, *'Abba*! Father!'" This knowledge of faith is possible only in the Holy Spirit: to be in touch with Christ, we must first have been touched by the Holy Spirit. He comes to meet us and kindles faith in us. By virtue of our Baptism, the first sacrament of the faith, the Holy Spirit in the Church communicates to us, intimately and personally, the life that originates in the Father and is offered to us in the Son. *Baptism gives us the grace of new birth in God the Father, through his Son, in the Holy Spirit. For those who bear God's Spirit are led to the Word, that is, to the Son, and the Son presents them to* *the Father, and the Father confers incorruptibility on them. And it is impossible to see God's Son without the Spirit, and no one can approach the Father without the Son, for the knowledge of the Father is the Son, and the knowledge of God's Son is obtained through the Holy Spirit.* — St. Irenaeus

Journal.

I BELIEVE IN THE ONE, HOLY, CATHOLIC, AND APOSTOLIC CHURCH

Colossians 1:15-20. He is the image of the invisible God, the firstborn of all creation. For in him were created all things in heaven and on earth, the visible and the invisible, whether thrones or dominions or principalities or powers, all things were created through him and for him. He is before all things, and in him all things hold together. He is the head of the body, the church. He is the beginning, the firstborn from the dead, that in all things he himself might be preeminent. For in him all the fullness was pleased to dwell, and through him to reconcile all things for him, making peace by the blood of his cross [through him], whether those on earth or those in heaven.

778. The Church is both the means and the goal of God's plan: prefigured in creation, prepared for in the Old Covenant, founded by the words and actions of Jesus Christ, fulfilled by his redeeming cross and his Resurrection, the Church has been manifested as the mystery of salvation by the outpouring of the Holy Spirit. She will be perfected in the glory of heaven as the assembly of all the redeemed of the earth (cf. *Rev* 14:4).

779. The Church is both visible and spiritual, a hierarchical society and the Mystical Body of Christ. She is one, yet formed of two components, human and divine. That is her mystery, which only faith can accept.

780. The Church in this world is the sacrament of salvation, the sign and the instrument of the communion of God and men.

Journal.

THE COMMUNION OF SAINTS

Hebrews 12:1-4. Therefore, since we are surrounded by so great a cloud of witnesses, let us rid ourselves of every burden and sin that clings to us and persevere in running the race that lies before us while keeping our eyes fixed on Jesus, the leader and perfecter of faith. For the sake of the joy that lay before him he endured the cross, despising its shame, and has taken his seat at the right of the throne of God. Consider how he endured such opposition from sinners, in order that you may not grow weary and lose heart. In your struggle against sin you have not yet resisted to the point of shedding blood.

946. After confessing "the holy catholic Church," the Apostles' Creed adds "the communion of saints." In a certain sense this article is a further explanation of the preceding: "What is the Church if not the assembly of all the saints?" The communion of saints is the Church.

962. "We believe in the communion of all the faithful of Christ, those who are pilgrims on earth, the dead who are being purified, and the blessed in heaven, all together forming one Church; and we believe that in this communion, the merciful love of God and his saints is always [attentive] to our prayers"

Journal.

THE FORGIVENESS OF SINS

John 20:20-23. When he had said this, he showed them his hands and his side. The disciples rejoiced when they saw the Lord. [Jesus] said to them again, "Peace be with you. As the Father has sent me, so I send you." And when he had said this, he breathed on them and said to them, "Receive the holy Spirit. Whose sins you forgive are forgiven them, and whose sins you retain are retained."

984. The Creed links "the forgiveness of sins" with its profession of faith in the Holy Spirit, for the risen Christ entrusted to the apostles the power to forgive sins when he gave them the Holy Spirit.

985. Baptism is the first and chief sacrament of the forgiveness of sins: it unites us to Christ, who died and rose, and gives us the Holy Spirit.

986. By Christ's will, the Church possesses the power to forgive the sins of the baptized and exercises it through bishops and priests normally in the sacrament of Penance.

Journal.

RESURRECTION OF THE DEAD

John 6:25-34. Amen, amen, I say to you, whoever hears my word and believes in the one who sent me has eternal life and will not come to condemnation, but has passed from death to life. Amen, amen, I say to you, the hour is coming and is now here when the dead will hear the voice of the Son of God, and those who hear will live. For just as the Father has life in himself, so also he gave to his Son the possession of life in himself. And he gave him power to exercise judgment, because he is the Son of Man. Do not be amazed at this, because the hour is coming in which all who are in the tombs will hear his voice and will come out, those who have done good deeds to the resurrection of life, but those who have done wicked deeds to the resurrection of condemnation.

989. We firmly believe, and hence we hope that, just as Christ is truly risen from the dead and lives for ever, so after death the righteous will live for ever with the risen Christ and he will raise them up on the last day. Our resurrection, like his own, will be the work of the Most Holy Trinity:

If the Spirit of him who raised Jesus from the dead dwells in you, he who raised Christ Jesus from the dead will give life to your mortal bodies also through his Spirit who dwells in you.

998. *Who will rise?* All the dead will rise, "those who have done good, to the resurrection of life, and those who have done evil, to the resurrection of judgment."

Journal.

DEATH

Luke 23:39-43. Now one of the criminals hanging there reviled Jesus, saying, "Are you not the Messiah? Save yourself and us." The other, however, rebuking him, said in reply, "Have you no fear of God, for you are subject to the same condemnation? And indeed, we have been condemned justly, for the sentence we received corresponds to our crimes, but this man has done nothing criminal." Then he said, "Jesus, remember me when you come into your kingdom." He replied to him, "Amen, I say to you, today you will be with me in Paradise."

1020. The Christian who unites his own death to that of Jesus views it as a step towards him and an entrance into everlasting life. When the Church for the last time speaks Christ's words of pardon and absolution over the dying Christian, seals him for the last time with a strengthening anointing, and gives him Christ in viaticum as nourishment for the journey, she speaks with gentle assurance:

Go forth, Christian soul, from this world
in the name of God the almighty Father,
who created you,

in the name of Jesus Christ, the Son of the living God,
who suffered for you,
in the name of the Holy Spirit,
who was poured out upon you.
Go forth, faithful Christian!
May you live in peace this day,
may your home be with God in Zion,
with Mary, the virgin Mother of God,
with Joseph, and all the angels and saints. ...
May you return to [your Creator]
who formed you from the dust of the earth.
May holy Mary, the angels, and all the saints
come to meet you as you go forth from this life. ...
May you see your Redeemer face to face.
– OCF, Prayer of Commendation

Journal.

HEAVEN

Revelation 22:1-5. Then the angel showed me the river of life-giving water, sparkling like crystal, flowing from the throne of God and of the Lamb down the middle of its street. On either side of the river grew the tree of life that produces fruit twelve times a year, once each month; the leaves of the trees serve as medicine for the nations. Nothing accursed will be found there anymore. The throne of God and of the Lamb will be in it, and his servants will worship him. They will look upon his face, and his name will be on their foreheads. Night will be no more, nor will they need light from lamp or sun, for the Lord God shall give them light, and they shall reign forever and ever.

1045. *For man*, this consummation will be the final realization of the unity of the human race, which God willed from creation and of which the pilgrim Church has been "in the nature of sacrament." Those who are united with Christ will form the community of the redeemed, "the holy city" of God, "the Bride, the wife of the Lamb." She will not be wounded any longer by sin, stains, self-love, that destroy or wound the earthly community. The beatific vision, in which God opens himself in an inexhaustible way to the elect, will be the ever-flowing well-spring of happiness, peace, and mutual communion.

Journal.

PURGATORY

2 Maccabees 12:38-46. Judas rallied his army and went to the city of Adullam. ... On the following day, since the task had now become urgent, Judas and his companions went to gather up the bodies of the fallen and bury them with their kindred in their ancestral tombs. But under the tunic of each of the dead they found amulets sacred to the idols of Jamnia, which the law forbids the Jews to wear. So it was clear to all that this was why these men had fallen. ...

Turning to supplication, they prayed that the sinful deed might be fully blotted out. ... He then took up a collection among all his soldiers, amounting to two thousand silver drachmas, which he sent to Jerusalem to provide for an expiatory sacrifice.

In doing this he acted in a very excellent and noble way, inasmuch as he had the resurrection in mind; for if he were not expecting the fallen to rise again, it would have been superfluous and foolish to pray for the dead.

But if he did this with a view to the splendid reward that awaits those who had gone to rest in godliness, it was a holy and pious thought. Thus he made atonement for the dead that they might be absolved from their sin.

1054. Those who die in God's grace and friendship imperfectly purified, although they are assured of their eternal salvation, undergo a purification after death, so as to achieve the holiness necessary to enter the joy of God.

Journal.

HELL

Matthew 13:36-43. Then, dismissing the crowds, he went into the house. His disciples approached him and said, "Explain to us the parable of the weeds in the field." He said in reply, "He who sows good seed is the Son of Man, the field is the world, the good seed the children of the kingdom. The weeds are the children of the evil one, and the enemy who sows them is the devil. The harvest is the end of the age, and the harvesters are angels. Just as weeds are collected and burned [up] with fire, so will it be at the end of the age.

The Son of Man will send his angels, and they will collect out of his kingdom all who cause others to sin and all evildoers. They will throw them into the fiery furnace, where there will be wailing and grinding of teeth. Then the righteous will shine like the sun in the kingdom of their Father. Whoever has ears ought to hear.

1033. We cannot be united with God unless we freely choose to love him. But we cannot love God if we sin gravely against him, against our neighbor or against ourselves: "He who does not love remains in death. Anyone

59

who hates his brother is a murderer, and you know that no murderer has eternal life abiding in him." Our Lord warns us that we shall be separated from him if we fail to meet the serious needs of the poor and the little ones who are his brethren. To die in mortal sin without repenting and accepting God's merciful love means remaining separated from him for ever by our own free choice. This state of definitive self-exclusion from communion with God and the blessed is called "hell."

Journal.

THE LAST JUDGEMENT

Matthew 25:31-46. "When the Son of Man comes in his glory, and all the angels with him, he will sit upon his glorious throne, and all the nations will be assembled before him. And he will separate them one from another, as a shepherd separates the sheep from the goats. He will place the sheep on his right and the goats on his left.

Then the king will say to those on his right, 'Come, you who are blessed by my Father. Inherit the kingdom prepared for you from the foundation of the world. For I was hungry and you gave me food, I was thirsty and you gave me drink, a stranger and you welcomed me, naked and you clothed me, ill and you cared for me, in prison and you visited me.' Then the righteous will answer him and say, 'Lord, when did we see you hungry and feed you, or thirsty and give you drink? When did we see you a stranger and welcome you, or naked and clothe you? When did we see you ill or in prison, and visit you?' And the king will say to them in reply, 'Amen, I say to you, whatever you did for one of these least brothers of mine, you did for me.'

Then he will say to those on his left, 'Depart from me, you

accursed, into the eternal fire prepared for the devil and his angels. For I was hungry and you gave me no food, I was thirsty and you gave me no drink, a stranger and you gave me no welcome, naked and you gave me no clothing, ill and in prison, and you did not care for me.' Then they will answer and say, 'Lord, when did we see you hungry or thirsty or a stranger or naked or ill or in prison, and not minister to your needs?'

He will answer them, 'Amen, I say to you, what you did not do for one of these least ones, you did not do for me.' And these will go off to eternal punishment, but the righteous to eternal life."

1040. The Last Judgment will come when Christ returns in glory. Only the Father knows the day and the hour; only he determines the moment of its coming. Then through his Son Jesus Christ he will pronounce the final word on all history. We shall know the ultimate meaning of the whole work of creation and of the entire economy of salvation and understand the marvelous ways by which his Providence led everything towards its final end. The Last Judgment will reveal that God's justice triumphs over all the injustices committed by his creatures and that God's love is stronger than death.

Journal.

"AMEN"

Revelation 22:16-21. "I, Jesus, sent my angel to give you this testimony for the churches. I am the root and offspring of David, the bright morning star." The Spirit and the bride say, "Come." Let the hearer say, "Come." Let the one who thirsts come forward, and the one who wants it receive the gift of life-giving water. ... The one who gives this testimony says, "Yes, I am coming soon."

Amen! Come, Lord Jesus!
The grace of the Lord Jesus be with all.

1062. In Hebrew, amen comes from the same root as the word "believe."

This root expresses solidity, trustworthiness, faithfulness. And so we can understand why "Amen" may express both God's faithfulness towards us and our trust in him.

1064. Thus the Creed's final "Amen" repeats and confirms its first words: "I believe." To believe is to say "Amen" to God's words, promises and commandments; to entrust oneself completely to him who is the "Amen" of infinite love and perfect faithfulness. The Christian's everyday life will then be the "Amen" to the "I believe" of our baptismal profession of faith

1065. Jesus Christ himself is the "Amen." He is the definitive "Amen" of the Father's love for us. He takes up and completes our "Amen" to the Father: "For all the promises of God find their Yes in him. That is why we utter the Amen through him, to the glory of God":

Through him, with him, in him,
in the unity of the Holy Spirit,
all glory and honor is yours,
almighty Father,
God, for ever and ever.
AMEN.

Journal.

SUNDAY GOSPELS WITH CATECHISM REFERENCES FOR THE THREE YEAR CYCLE

CYCLE A – "Year of St. Matthew"

First Sunday of Advent	Matthew 24:37-44	673
Second Sunday of Advent	Matthew 3:1-12	523, 535, 678
Immaculate Conception	Luke 1:26-38	497, 706, 723, 2571
Third Sunday of Advent	Matthew 11:2-11	548, 549, 2443
Fourth Sunday of Advent	Matthew 1:18-24	497
Birth of Our Lord	*Vigil*– Matthew 1:1-25 or 1:18-25	437, 497, 744, 2812
	Midnight– Luke 2:1-14	333, 437, 448, 695, 725
	Dawn– Luke 2:15-20	2599
	Day– John 1:1-18 or 1:1-5, 9-14	291, 454, 496, 505, 594, 612, 705, 717-19, 1996, 2466
Holy Family	Matthew 2:13-15, 19-23	333, 530
Mary, Mother of God	Luke 2:16-21	333, 527, 2599
Second Sunday after Christmas	John 1:1-18 or 1:1-5, 9-14	291, 445, 473, 706, 1996
Epiphany of the Lord	Matthew 2:1-12	486
Baptism of the Lord	Matthew 3:13-17	535, 1286
Second Sunday in Ordinary Time	John 1:29-34	408, 438, 486, 523, 536, 608, 713, 1137, 1505
Third Sunday in Ordinary Time	Matthew 4:12-23 or 4:12-17	878, 1720, 1989
Fourth Sunday in Ordinary Time	Matthew 5:1-12a	520, 544, 581, 1716, 1720, 2518, 2546
Fifth Sunday in Ordinary Time	Matthew 5:13-16	782, 2821
Sixth Sunday in Ordinary Time	Matthew 5:17-37 or Matthew 5:20-22a, 27-28, 33-34a, 37	577, 592, 1424, 1967, 2053, 2054
Annunciation	Luke 1:26-28	497, 706, 723, 2571
Ash Wednesday	Matthew 6:1-6, 16-18	1430, 1434, 1969

First Sunday of Lent	Matthew 4:1-11	394, 2849
Second Sunday of Lent	Matthew 17:1-9	444, 554
Third Sunday of Lent	John 4:5-42 or John 4:5-15, 19b-26, 39a, 40-42	544, 586, 728, 2560, 2561
Fourth Sunday of Lent	John 9:1-41 or John 9:1, 6-9, 13-17, 34-38	588, 596, 1151, 1504, 2173
Fifth Sunday of Lent	John 11:1-45 or John 11:3-7, 17,20-27, 33b-45	472, 581, 627, 640, 994, 1001, 2604
Passion / Palm Sunday	Matthew 26:14-27:66 or Matthew 27:11-54	363, 536, 585, 596-7, 612, 764, 1403, 2719, 2849
Mass of Chrism	Luke 4:16-21	436, 1286
Mass of the Lord's Supper	John 13:1-15	557, 609, 616, 622, 1694, 1823
Good Friday	John 18:1 to 19:42	217, 440, 501, 559, 586, 596, 600, 607-9
Easter Vigil	Matthew 28:1-10	500, 641, 652, 2174
Easter Sunday	John 20:1-9	333, 515, 640, 641, 652, 2174
Easter Sunday Evening	Luke 24:13-35	1329, 1347
Second Sunday of Easter or Divine Mercy Sunday	John 20:19-31	575, 643-5, 659
Third Sunday of Easter	Luke 24:13-35	1329, 1347
Fourth Sunday of Easter	John 10:1-10	754
Fifth Sunday of Easter	John 14:1-12	74, 151, 459, 470, 661, 1025, 1698, 2795
Sixth Sunday of Easter	John 14:15-21	243, 687, 692, 2466, 2615, 2671
Ascension of the Lord	Matthew 28:16-20	645, 857, 1444
Seventh Sunday of Easter	John 17:1-11a	217, 730, 1069, 1085, 2747-51, 2812
Pentecost Sunday Vigil	John 7:37-39	728, 1287, 1999, 2561
Pentecost Sunday	John 20:19-23 or 5:26-27	575, 643-5, 659, 694, 976, 1461, 2839

70

Solemnity of the Most Holy Trinity	John 3:16-18	219, 444, 454, 458, 679, 706
Solemnity of the Most Holy Body and Blood of Christ	John 6:51-58	728, 1355, 1384, 1406, 1509, 2837
Solemnity of the Most Sacred Heart of Jesus	Matthew 11:25-30	153, 544, 1615, 2603, 2701, 2779, 2785
Seventh Sunday in Ordinary Time	Matthew 5:38-48	1825, 1933, 1968, 2262, 2303, 2443, 2608, 2844,
Eighth Sunday in Ordinary Time	Matthew 6:24-34	322, 2113, 2424, 2547, 2729, 2830
Ninth Sunday in Ordinary Time	Matthew 7:21-27	1970
Tenth Sunday in Ordinary Time	Matthew 9:9-13	581, 589, 2100
Eleventh Sunday in Ordinary Time	Matthew 9:36 -10:8	543, 1509, 2121, 2443, 2611
Twelfth Sunday in Ordinary Time	Matthew 10:26-33	305, 363, 765, 1034, 1215, 1816
Thirteenth Sunday in Ordinary Time	Matthew 10:37-42	858, 1506, 2232
Fourteenth Sunday in Ordinary Time	Matthew 11:25-30	151, 443, 459, 473, 544, 1658, 2701, 2779, 2785
Fifteenth Sunday in Ordinary Time	Matthew 13:1-23 or Matthew 13:1-9	29, 546, 787, 1724
Sixteenth Sunday in Ordinary Time	Matthew 13:24-43 or Matthew 13:24-30	333, 837, 1034
Seventeenth Sunday in Ordinary Time	Matthew 13:44-52 or Matthew 13:44-46	546, 1034, 1117
Eighteenth Sunday in Ordinary Time	Matthew 14:13-21	1335
Nineteenth Sunday in Ordinary Time	Matthew 14:22-23	448
Assumption Vigil	Luke 11:27-28	None cited

Assumption of Mary	Luke 1:39-56	148, 448, 523, 717, 722, 2619, 2675, 2676, 2677
Twentieth Sunday in Ordinary Time	Matthew 15:21-28	439, 448, 2610
Twenty-first Sunday in Ordinary Time	Matthew 16:13-20	153, 424, 440, 442, 552, 553, 869, 881, 1444.
Twenty-second Sunday in Ordinary Time	Matthew 16:21-27	226, 363, 540, 554, 607, 618, 736
Twenty-third Sunday in Ordinary Time	Matthew 18:15-20	553, 1088, 1373, 1444, 2472
The Exultation of the Holy Cross	John 3:13-17	219, 444, 454, 458, 679, 706, 2130
Twenty-fourth Sunday in Ordinary Time	Matthew 18:21-35	982, 2227, 2845, 2843
Twenty-fifth Sunday in Ordinary Time	Matthew *20:*1-16a	None cited
Twenty-sixth Sunday in Ordinary Time	Matthew 21:28-32	535, 546
Twenty-seventh Sunday in Ordinary Time	Matthew 21:33-43	443, 755, 756
Twenty-eighth Sunday in Ordinary Time	Matthew 22:1-14 or Matthew 22:1-10	546, 796
Twenty-ninth Sunday in Ordinary Time	Matthew 22:15-21	2242
Thirtieth Sunday in Ordinary Time	Matthew 22:34-40	581, 1824, 2055, 2083
Thirty-first Sunday in Ordinary Time	Matthew 23:1-12	526, 2367
Thirty-second Sunday in Ordinary Time	Matthew 25:1-13 Matthew 24:14-15, 19-21	672, 796, 1618
Christ the King	Matthew 25:31-46	544, 1033, 1373, 2443, 2447, 2831

CYCLE B – "Year of St. Mark"

First Sunday of Advent	Mark 13:33-37	672, 2849
Second Sunday of Advent	Mark 1:1-8	422, 515
Immaculate Conception	Luke 1: 26-38	497, 706, 723, 2571
Third Sunday of Advent	John 1:6-8, 19-28	717, 719, 1216
Fourth Sunday of Advent	Luke 1:26-38	497, 706, 723
Birth of Our Lord	*Vigil*-- Matt 1:1-25 or 1:18-25	437, 497, 744, 2812
	Midnight-- Luke 2:1-14	333, 437, 448, 695, 725
	Dawn-- Luke 2:15-20	2599
	Day-- John 1:1-18 or 1:1-5, 9-14	291, 454, 496, 505, 594, 612, 705, 717-19, 1996, 2466
Holy Family	Luke 2:22-40 or Luke 2:22, 39-40	
Mary, Mother of God	Luke 2:16-21	527, 2599
Second Sunday after Christmas	John 1:1-18 or 1:1-5,9-4	291, 445, 473, 706, 1996
Epiphany of the Lord	Matthew 2:1-12	486
Baptism of the Lord	Mark 1:7-11	151, 422
Second Sunday in Ordinary Time	John 1:35-42	608
Third Sunday in Ordinary Time	Mark 1:14-20	541, 787, 1427
Fourth Sunday in Ordinary Time	Mark 1:21-28	438, 1673, 2173
Presentation of the Lord	Luke 2:22-40	529, 583
Fifth Sunday in Ordinary Time	Mark 1:29-39	2602
Sixth Sunday in Ordinary Time	Mark 1:40-45	1504, 2616
Seventh Sunday in Ordinary Time	Mark 2:2-12	1421

Eighth Sunday in Ordinary Time	Mark 2:18-22	796
Ninth Sunday in Ordinary Time	Mark 2:23- 3:6 or Mark 2:23-28	544, 574, 581, 582, 2167, 2173
Annunciation	Luke 1:26-38	497, 706, 723, 2571
First Sunday of Lent	Mark 1:12-15	538
Second Sunday of Lent	Mark 9:2-10	151, 459, 552
Third Sunday of Lent	John 2:13-25 [A] John 4:5...42	473, 575, 583-6, 994 [A] 439, 606, 1179, 2824
Fourth Sunday of Lent	John 3:14-21	219, 444, 679, 706, 2130
	[A] John 9:1...38	[A] 595, 1151, 1504, 2827
Fifth Sunday of Lent	John 12:20-33	363, 434, 607, 2731
	[A]John 11:1-45	[A] 439, 581, 994, 1001
Passion / Palm Sunday	Mark 14:1 to 15:47 or Mark 15:1-39	473-4, 1335, 1339, 1403
Mass of Chrism	Luke 4:16-21	436
Mass of the Lord's Supper	John 13:1-15	557, 609, 616, etc.
Good Friday	John 18:1 to 19:42	607, 624, 596, 2471, etc.
Easter Vigil	Mark 16:1-7	952
Easter Sunday	10hn 20:1-9	952
Easter Sunday Evening	Luke 24:13-35	1329, 1347
Second Sunday of Easter or Divine Mercy Sunday	John 20:19-31	575, 643, 1287, 1485
Third Sunday of Easter	Luke 24:35-48	644, 645, 999
Fourth Sunday of Easter	John 10:11-18	754
Fifth Sunday of Easter	John 15:1-8	308, 755, 787, 859, 864, 1108, 1694, 2074
Sixth Sunday of Easter	John 15:9-17	1824, 1970, 2745
Ascension of the Lord	Mark 16:15-20	523, 2832
Seventh Sunday of Easter	John 17:llb-19	2747-2750

Pentecost Vigil	John 7:37-39	728, 1287, 2561
Pentecost Sunday	John 20:19-23 or	575, 643-5, 1087
	John 15:26-27	263, 729, 1287, 2671
Solemnity of the Most Holy Trinity	Matt 28:16-20	857, 1444
Solemnity of the Most Holy Body and Blood of Christ	Mark 14:12-16, 22-26	474
Solemnity of the Most Sacred Heart of Jesus	John 19:31-37	None cited
Tenth Sunday in Ordinary Time	Mark 3:20-35	500, 539, 548, 574, 1874
Eleventh Sunday in Ordinary Time	Mark 4:26-34	548
Twelfth Sunday in Ordinary Time	Mark 4:35-41	None cited
Saints Peter and Paul	Matt 16:13-19	153, 424, 440, 442, 881, 1969
Thirteenth Sunday in Ordinary Time	Mark 5:21-43 or Mark 5:21-24, 35b-43	994
Fourteenth Sunday in Ordinary Time	Mark 6:1-6	500, 699, 2610
Fifteenth Sunday in Ordinary Time	Mark 6:7-13	765, 1506, 1673
Sixteenth Sunday in Ordinary Time	Mark 6:30-34	None cited
Seventeenth Sunday in Ordinary Time	John 6:1-15	439, 549, 559, 1338
Eighteenth Sunday in Ordinary Time	John 6:24-35	2835
Nineteen Sunday in Ordinary Time	John 6:41-51	2835
Assumption Vigil	Luke 11:27-28	None cited

Assumption of Mary	Luke 1:39-56	523, 717, 722, 2619, 2675
Twentieth Sunday in Ordinary Time	John 6:51-58	728, 1355, 1406, 2837, 1384
Twenty-first Sunday in Ordinary Time	John 6:60-69	438, 473, 728, 1336
Twenty-second Sunday in Ordinary Time	Mark 7:1-8, 14-15,21-23	574, 581
Twenty-third Sunday in Ordinary Time	Mark 7:31-37	1151, 1504
The Exultation of the Holy Cross	John 3:13-17	423, 440, 444, 458, 661, 679
Twenty-fourth Sunday in Ordinary Time	Mark 8:27-35	459, 472, 474, 557, 649, 1615
Twenty-fifth Sunday in Ordinary Time	Mark 9:30-37	1825
Twenty-sixth Sunday in Ordinary Time	Mark 9:38-43,45,47-48	1034
Twenty-seventh Sunday in Ordinary Time	Mark 10:2-16 or Mark 10:2-12	699, 1627-39, 2364, 2382
Twenty-eighth Sunday in Ordinary Time	Mark 10:17-30 or Mark 10:17-27	1618, 1858,2728
Twenty-ninth Sunday in Ordinary Time	Mark 10:35- 45 or Mark 10:42-45	536, 608, 618, 1225, 1551, 570
Thirtieth Sunday in Ordinary Time	Mark 10:46-52	548, 2616, 2667
All Souls	John 6:37-40	606, 989, 1001, 2824
Dedication of the Basilica of St. John Lateran, Rome	John 2:13-22	575, 586, 994, 5833
Thirty-first Sunday in Ordinary Time	Mark 12:28b-34	129, 202, 228, 575, 2196
Thirty-second Sunday in Ordinary Time	Mark 12:38-44 or Mark 12:41-44	678, 2444

Thirty-third Sunday in Ordinary Time	Mark 13:24-32	474, 673, 2612
Christ the King	John 18:33b-37	217, 549, 559, 600, 2471

CYCLE C – "The Year of St. Luke"

First Sunday of Advent	Luke 21:25-28, 34-36	586,716,746,972,612
Second Sunday of Advent	Luke 3:1-6	535
Immaculate Conception	Luke 1:26-38	4,884,977,067,232,570
Third Sunday of Advent	Luke 3:10-18	5,356,962,447
Fourth Sunday of Advent	Luke 1:39-45	1,485,237,172,676
Birth of Our Lord	*Vigil*-- Matt 1:1-25 or 1:18-25	437, 497, 744, 2812
	Midnight-- Luke 2:1-14	333, 437, 448, 695, 725
	Dawn-- Luke 2:15-20	2599
	Day-- John 1:1-18 or 1:1-5, 9-14	291, 454, 496, 505, 594, 612, 705, 717-9, 1996, 2466
Holy Family	Luke 2:41-52	534
Mary, Mother of God	Luke 2:16-21	527, 2599
Second Sunday after Christmas	John 1:1-18	268, 291, 454, 717-9, 1996
Epiphany of the Lord	Matthew 2:1-12	439, 486, 528, 724
Baptism of the Lord	Luke 3:15-16,21-22	696
Second Sunday in Ordinary Time	John 2:1-11	486, 495, 1335, 1613, 2618
Third Sunday in Ordinary Time	Luke 1:1-4 and 4:14-21	436, 544, 695, 714, 1168, 1286. 2443
Fourth Sunday in Ordinary Time	Luke 4:21-30	436
Fifth Sunday in Ordinary Time	Luke 5:1-11	208
Sixth Sunday in Ordinary Time	Luke 6:17,20-26	244,425,462,547
Ash Wednesday	Matthew 6:1-6, 16-18	1063, 1430, 1434, 1969, 1753, 2447, 2759,
First Sunday of Lent	Luke 4:1-13	538, 695, 2096, 2119, 2855

81

Second Sunday of Lent	Luke 9:28b-36	550
Third Sunday of Lent	Luke 13:1-9	None cited
	[A] John 4:5-42	[A] 1439, 606, 1179, 2824
	[A] John 9:1-38	[Al 595, 1151, 1504, 2824
Fifth Sunday of Lent	John 8:1-11	583
	[A] John 11:1-45	[Al 439,581,994, 1001
Passion / Palm Sunday	Luke 22:14 - 23:56 or Luke 23:1-49	333, 550, 591-7, 607, 1130, 1403, 1570, 2804
Mass of Chrism	Luke 4:16-21	436, 1286
Mass of the Lord's Supper	John 13:1-15	557, 609, 616 622, 1694, 1823.
Good Friday	John 18:1 to 19:42	217, 440, 501, 559, 586, 596, 600, 607-9
Easter Vigil	Luke 24:1-12	626, 640, 641, 643, 652, 2174
Easter Sunday	John 20:1-9	452
Easter Sunday Evening	Luke 24:13-35	1329, 1347
Second Sunday of Easter or Divine Mercy Sunday	John 20:19-31	442, 448, 514, 644, 788, 1087
Third Sunday of Easter	John 21:1-19 or John 21:1-14	448, 553, 618, 645, 659, 881, 1429, 1551
Fourth Sunday of Easter	John 10:27-30	548, 582, 590
Fifth Sunday of Easter	John 13:31-31a, 34-35	782, 1823, 1970, 2195, 2822, 2842
Sixth Sunday of Easter	John 14:23-29	243, 244, 263, 692, 729, 1099, 2466, 2623
Ascension of the Lord	Luke 24:46-53	627, 659, 730, 981, 1120, 1122
Seventh Sunday of Easter	John 17:20-26	244, 260, 690, 820, 877, 2750.
Pentecost Sunday Vigil	John 20:19-23	575, 643-5, 659, 976, 1461, 2839,
Pentecost Sunday	John 14:15-16, 23b-26	692, 729, 2615
Solemnity of the Most Holy Trinity	John 16:12-15	91, 243, 244, 485, 687, 690, 692, 1117, 2466, 2615, 2671

Solemnity of the Most Holy Body & Blood of Christ	Luke 9:11 b-17	None cited
Solemnity of the Most Sacred Heart of Jesus	Luke 15:3-7	545
Seventh Sunday in Ordinary Time	Luke 6:27-38	1458, 1069, 1789, 1970, 2842
Eighth Sunday in Ordinary Time	Luke 6:39-45	None cited
Ninth Sunday in Ordinary Time	Luke 7:1-10	None cited
Tenth Sunday in Ordinary Time	Luke 7:11-17	994
Eleventh Sunday in Ordinary Time	Luke 7:36 - 8:3 or Luke 7:36-50	575, 588, 1441, 2616
Twelfth Sunday in Ordinary Time	Luke 9:18-24	1435, 2600
Thirteenth Sunday in Ordinary Time	Luke 9:51-62	544, 557
Fourteenth Sunday in Ordinary Time	Luke 10:1-12, 17-20 or Luke 10:1-9	87, 765, 787, 2122, 2611
Fifteenth Sunday in Ordinary Time	Luke 10:25-37	1825, 2083, 2822
Sixteenth Sunday in Ordinary Time	Luke 10:38-42	None cited
Seventeenth Sunday in Ordinary Time	Luke 11:1-13	520, 1425, 2601, 2613, 2632, 2759, 2845
Eighteenth Sunday in Ordinary Time	Luke 12:13-31	549
Nineteenth Sunday in Ordinary Time	Luke 12:32-48	764, 2849
Assumption Vigil	Luke 11:27-28	None cited
Assumption of Mary	Luke 1:39-56	523, 717, 722, 2619, 2675

Twentieth Sunday in Ordinary Time	Luke 12:49-53	536, 607, 696, 1225; 2804
Twenty-first Sunday in Ordinary Time	Luke 13:22-30	2660
Twenty-second Sunday in Ordinary Time	Luke 14:1,7-14	575, 588
Twenty-third Sunday in Ordinary Time	Luke 14:25-33	1618, 2544
The Exultation of the Holy Cross	John 3:13-17	423, 440, 444, 458, 661, 679
Twenty-fourth Sunday in Ordinary Time	Luke 15:1-32 or Luke 15:1-10	545, 589, 1423, 1439, 1468, 1700, 2795, 2839
Thirty-first Sunday in Ordinary Time	Luke 19:1-10	549, 1443, 2412, 2712
Thirty-third Sunday in Ordinary Time	Luke 21:5-19	675
Christ the King	Luke 23:35-43	440, 1021, 2266,2616

CONTINUE THE MEDITATIONS

This is the first of a four book series meant to give 30 daily meditations from each pillar of the Catechism of the Catholic Church.

- **01. The Profession of Faith**
- **02. The Celebration of the Christian Mystery**
- **03. Life in Christ**
- **04. Christian Prayer**

To order the next book or for bulk orders visit the site:

www.reverbculture.com/meditationsbook

LEARN TO PRAY WITH THE CATECHISM AND SCRIPTURE

Dual Wielding: A Guide to Praying with the Catechism and Scripture is a book written to help you learn to pray with the two most important books any Catholic could own and use in prayer. This book was lovingly crafted to not just teach you, but also help you fall in love with Jesus through the Catechism and Scripture in a way you never thought possible.

You'll be able to take what might seem like a dry and overly technical book and use it in prayer to discover the heart of God and make Scripture come to life.

To purchase the book and the cocktail recipes, guided reflections, printable resources, videos, and more visit:

www.reverbculture.com/dualwield

ABOUT REVERB CULTURE

Reverb Culture is an online community of Catholics committed to living the life of wild orthodoxy.

Join the community at:

www.ReverbCulture.com

Journal.

Journal.

Journal.

Journal.

Journal.

Journal.

Journal.

Journal.

Journal.

Journal.

Journal.

Journal.

Journal.

35579727R00066

Made in the USA
Middletown, DE
07 October 2016